The Art of Influence

By Landon T. Smith

Table of Contents

Introduction

Influence! We all need it, we all want it, but not many of us understand just what exactly it is. To some people influence is seen as some kind of mystical power that can be exuded on others, allowing you to control those within your reach. Some see influence as some kind of charisma, but the reality is that influence is just simply defined as the ability to have an effect on someone else. This definition is broad, but that's a good thing. The truth is that we all influence people in our lives on a daily basis. We all have an effect on other people, no matter what we do.

The point of this book is to take a look at what kind of effect that we want to have on others. Do we want to be able to effectively persuade other people? Do we want to be able to affect people for the better? When we say that someone is influential, what we really mean is that they are able to influence people for the better. The most influential people in society are those who are capable of enacting a great deal of change in others, so much so that it has had an influence on the world itself.

The question isn't how can I be influential, the question is: how can I be effective with the influence that I have? How can I get the results that I want with my influence? The more you focus on increasing your ability to affect other people, the greater your influence on them will be. So, the focus of this book isn't about giving you quick and clever tricks that will help you manipulate people, rather the focus of this book will be to help you understand how influence works, how to increase the results from our own influence and most importantly, how to improve your own influence. If you've always wanted to be a more influential person, then get ready!

Chapter 1: Understanding Influence

The first step to being able to influence people is being able to understand how the mechanics of influence work. We tend to think of influence as some kind of supernatural force, something that will exude from your words or actions and end up convincing another person to do your bidding. As stated before, this is a fallacy and tends to come from the false idea that people can be somehow controlled by our words or actions.

The reality is that people are extremely in control of their own minds, thoughts and actions, so in truth, we don't have the ability to do some kind of clever manipulation tricks to make them do our bidding. What we do have, however, is the ability to *appeal* to them on various different levels. The basics of human motivation is extremely simplistic. People do what they want to do. Simple as that. There are ways to get a person to do something that they don't want to do, such as threatening them, coercing them, paying them or tricking them, but then again, that isn't influence at all. That is what is known as manipulation. Manipulation and influence are not the same at all. A person who influences others gets long lasting results from the people that they are influencing. Someone who chooses to manipulate others will only get short term results and will most likely end up dealing with the consequences of their unethical behavior later on. Essentially, if you are someone who wants to get the best deal for your efforts, then it is a much better idea to learn how to influence people instead of focusing on trying to manipulate them.

As stated before, people are entirely in control of their own actions. Many times, we can harbor the false belief that people are not rational actors, meaning that they do things without knowing why, they are controlled by their emotions and don't really have a free choice in what they do, but this belief is a flawed premise. No matter what a person is feeling, experiencing or thinking, they always have a choice when it comes to decision making. What happens is that many people try to explain that they have no choice in decision making as a way to escape from the responsibility of their own decisions. But these are nothing more than excuses. An excuse is not a reality. So, when someone says "I can't help it!" they actually can help it, but they are just giving in to an excuse.

Since people are rational actors and are in complete control over the decisions that they make, how then, do they make decisions? Why do people do the things that they do? This requires a simple understanding of human psychology and motivation. Essentially, people make decisions based on their beliefs. A belief is a long term understanding of how the world works, usually formed at different periods in a person's life. For example, when you sit in a chair, you believe that the chair will support your weight. You have no logical way of knowing that the chair will support you other than the fact that you have observed many times over your life the fact that the chair will support you. This is the basis of a belief, that the world works a certain kind of way.

So, all of our actions and decision making take our beliefs into account first. After the beliefs, come our emotions, understanding and logic. Beliefs and emotion have much more to do with decision making than logic and rationality do. This might seem somewhat backwards, but it is a reality. When someone believes that a decision will hurt them, it doesn't matter about any of the reality or truth, they will behave accordingly. For example, if someone is trying to get into a cold pool, they might be reticent to do so because they believe it is extremely painful to get into the cold water. The reality is that cold water is uncomfortable, but it is not painful. Yet when the person under the false belief must confront the truth, they will try to shape the current situation to match their own beliefs instead of adapting to a new way of thinking.

This can be summed up by an old joke. A man goes to see a psychiatrist and tells the doctor, "Doctor, I am a corpse. I died just a few days ago, and now I'm dead." The psychiatrist, seeing that the man is living and breathing says to the man "well, everyone knows that a corpse doesn't bleed, right?" "Of course," the man replies, "a corpse doesn't bleed!" Well, the psychiatrist, trying to prove a point to the man takes a needle and gently pricks the man's finger, causing a tiny droplet of blood to emerge. The man looks at the blood and says "Well I guess a corpse does bleed!"

When people are forced to confront things that challenge their beliefs, they tend to distort the facts so that it matches up with what they believe, *rather* than form new beliefs. Why? Well, the human brain is designed in such a way as to retain information and patterns and it's not particularly interested in deleting old information. So, when we experience things that challenge us, unless we desire to have an open mind and really look at those things, our beliefs do not change. We just react differently based on our beliefs.

After belief comes emotion. Our beliefs color how we see things, but our emotions color how we feel at any given moment. There are some people in this world who are primarily seen as very emotional creatures due to the fact that they are always crying or getting upset, then there are those who are seen as stoic and emotionless due to the fact that they don't display their emotions outwardly too much. The reality is that both of those kinds of people equally are emotional, they just display their emotions differently. People tend to respond to situations based on the way their emotions are driving them. Someone who is primarily in an angry emotion will respond with anger or irritation, someone who is happy might respond to things favorably.

After our emotions, comes logic and reasoning. We consider facts, but only after we are able to look at them without feeling afraid, threatened or having a conflict with our beliefs. This means that the majority of people in the world don't particularly change based on facts. They tend to change based on the way they feel about the facts. Those who are particularly well trained and who are open minded might be able to put their emotions aside as they pursue truth, but if someone is closed off to learning a new perspective, there are no amounts of facts that will change a person's mind. Only experiential things will help a person change their closed minds.

So, that's the short order of how people make decisions. Their beliefs color how they see the world, their emotions indicate their moods and actions, their understanding and reasoning ability finally lead them to make their decision. So where does influence come in? Well, it's based primarily on what motivates a person. People are motived by all sorts of different beliefs, but we can all essentially be summed up as motivated by our desire for Security and Significance.

Security is the idea of being safe. Most everyone wants to experience some form of safety, either being same from harm, pain or suffering. It is one of the most powerful things that drive humans forward, it is what causes a man to build a massive castle to defend himself, it is what makes a woman desire a large bank account. Everyone has different ideas of what makes them feel safe, for some people it is freedom, for others it can actually even be something like a day job. While people might disagree on what things make them feel safe, what everyone can agree on is that we all have an innate desire to feel safe on some level. Some people look at security on an external level, working hard to make the world around them safe, others might look for security inwardly, learning how to become strong and self-reliant in order to be as safe as possible. Most human interactions on a basic level can be seen as the quest for security. In the ancient times, it was the quest to find the perfect grounds to settle down and build a house, in modern times, it can be seen as the quest to get a college degree, a house and a 9-5 job. These motivations are present within every single human.

The second significant motivator within people is the search for Significance. People innately desire to have some kind of significance in the world. They want to feel loved, valid and valued. So much so that they are willing to do great acts of kindness and great acts of horror in order to gain those feelings. The man who wants to find love is seeking out significance, while the man who is looking for fame and fortune is also looking for the exact same kind of significance. Like safety, everyone has different ideas of what makes them feel significant, but we can all agree that we have a deep-seated desire to have significance in this world.

These two major motivators essentially capture the entirety of human motivation. Regardless of what a person is doing, their desires usually fall into one or both of those categories. People focus on inventing strategies in order to achieve these things. Those strategies are usually long term actions or goals. What happens in most people is that they confuse their strategy for being their motivator. For example, if someone wants to feel significant, they might come up with a strategy of having a successful business. Yet in their minds, they think they are motivated by the desire for a business, while the reality is that they are motivated by their desire for significance. The more we are able to understand the base psychology of what motivates a person to move forward, the more we are able to influence these people successfully.

If you want to learn how to influence people, then you must learn how to speak the language of influence. The language of influence is essentially being able to skip past the surface motivations in a person's mind and target the deeper motivations inside. It's about being able to inspire a person on a level that goes past the basics and inflames them from their very core. When you are able to speak to a person on that deep of a level, they will respond much differently than someone who is motivated by surface level desires and wants.

By learning a person's beliefs, desires, emotions and thoughts, you are able to essentially decipher their entire personhood. When you can identify what they believe will bring them security and safety, you are learning the building blocks that will allow for you to begin to affect them in a very powerful and long lasting way. The reality about influence is that it is a way for you to be able to get people to do what you want, but in order to get someone to do what you want, you have to first be able to offer something in return.

People often confused money for influence because money has the power to get someone to do what you want. Pretty much no matter what the task is, if you attach enough zeroes to the paycheck, you could get people to do your bidding. There are those in this world who think that in order to become an influential person, you must be rich, but there are millions of influential people in this world who have little to no money. While it is true that money can assist in creating the perception that you are influential, money doesn't really give you the power to influence anyone. It just gives you the power to motivate them through external means of control. A true test of influence is when you take money away from the situation, would that person still follow you? Would they still do as you asked? There are so many millionaires and billionaires in this world who would be up a creek without a paddle if they didn't have their money to command the loyalty of their followers.

Yet, there is something significantly more powerful than money out in this world: the ability to appeal to people's desires. Think of influential people like Martin Luther King Jr, a man who was able to command the loyalty of a great many, to sway the nation when it came to civil rights and get people to follow after his cause of desegregating the United States. Did he command loyalty because of the prestige offered by his cause? Were people being promised riches and glory? Not at all, they were being offered the opportunity to get involved with a cause that would very well take a long time to reach, but appealed greatly to many people's sense of either significance or security. They were so affected by his words that a great many were willing to go to prison, or travel a great length in order to protest the discrimination. Even those who were white followed King's lead, despite the fact that they had nothing to gain out of fighting for civil rights. All of that came not from money, but from the purest form of influence that can exist.

In order to be a strong influencer, you must be able to understand what moves and motivates a person. After that, it's just a matter of learning how to properly communicate to that person. Influence is one half understanding and one half communication. So many people assume that the best influencers have some clever way with words, but the truth is that the best influencers understand what drives a person and how to appeal to that drive.

So, the first step to being able to influence someone is being able to assess their motivations, emotions, feelings, beliefs and patterns. This isn't particularly easy to do from a distance, which brings us to our very first major step to influence, the Evaluation phase. Let's go over each step in detail so that you can learn how to understand people you are seeking to influence.

Evaluation Step One: Relationship

The first step to evaluating someone for the purpose of being able to increase your influence on them is to assess your relationship with them. Are you friends? Strangers? Estranged family? The kind of relationship that you have with a person can ultimately determine how you are able to affect them. It is easier to influence friends than family members, strangers than enemies and volunteers than employees. How a person sees you can ultimately determine what you are able to influence them to do. If they view you favorably, if they like you, it's easier to ask them for help or convey vision, if they view you unfavorably, then you're going to have to handle that first before you are able to increase your influence over them.

Evaluation Step Two: Behavior

When looking at the person or people that you are wanting to influence more, you must be able to make assumptions based off of their behavior. People don't behave randomly ever.

They have detailed understandings and beliefs that will cause them to act in a certain way. By learning to watch the actions that they undertake and make a series of educated guesses as to the motives behind their actions, you can begin to learn what ultimately motivates people. The more that you understand basic human motivation, the easier it will be to influence them later on.

Evaluation Step Three: Questioning

Believe it or not, but most people are actually very open to being asked questions about themselves. Most of us don't realize the immense power that we hold in our hands because we tend not to think of other people as very deep. If you are in the process of wanting to learn more about others, so that you can better understand how you can influence them for the better, you must be able to ask them questions about themselves. The more questions you ask, the easier it will be. It might feel a little uncomfortable at first, but if you are calm and interested when you ask a person some questions about their motivations, they usually end up talking quite a lot. This is far easier than guessing as to what a person's motivations would be. Now, most people won't tell you that they are searching for significance or security, so it's easier to get more information about their motivations by asking them "why?" When a person is asked "why do you think that?" or "what led you to that conclusion?" it often will reveal a great deal of information about themselves, so much so that they will tend to go even deeper than you expected.

Evaluation Step Four: Learn Temperaments

Everyone has a different temperament. A temperament is a person's natural, innate behavioral traits. Some people have very strong, aggressive temperaments, while others have very passive, gentle temperaments. We don't really have control over our temperaments themselves, we are born with them. While we learn to control aspects of our temperaments (such as learning not to get into fights if you are naturally an aggressive person) we never really change from our core selves. This is fine, of course, as no temperament is better than the others. The two core temperaments to understand right now are introversion and extroversion. An introvert is someone who naturally finds themselves attracted to isolation, being alone and are recharged by silence and rest. An extrovert is someone who prefers to be in a crowd of people and enjoys socialization, finding themselves being drained by their loneliness and isolation. When you can determine if a person is an extrovert or an introvert, it gives you the opportunity to learn how best to motivate them.

After you have learned how to understand and evaluate people for the sake of learning how to influence them, we must then learn what the purpose of influence is for.

Chapter 2: Influential Purposes

So, we've seen the fact that people are primarily driven by their own internal worlds, their emotions, beliefs and opinions primarily lead their decision-making process. Now we must begin to ask the question: why do you want to be influential? We must understand the purpose of being able to influence others in order to be able to do so effectively.

There are many reasons that a person would desire to be influential. Oftentimes, the reason is so that they can have some kind of power over other people. Many crave influence because they believe that it is the ticket to fulfilling their own needs for significance or security and in doing so, make many terrible mistakes. Everyone has a natural level of influence over others, meaning that we have the ability to affect people in our lives. When you ask a friend for a favor and they agree, it is because they consider your influence in their lives to be positive. When you begin to lead other people in your businesses and they begin to grow stronger and more capable under your leadership, it is because of your influence.

There can be positive influence on a person's life or there can be negative influences. When a boss pushes his employees too hard and they begin to experience stress due to his actions, he is having a negative influence on them. When a mother yells angrily at her children day in and day out, they begin to experience negative opinions, attitudes and emotions due to that influence. Essentially, our ability to influence people can be an extremely good thing or it can be a very bad thing. Just as there have been extremely good influential people, such as Gandhi, there can be heinous influential people, such as Charles Manson.

If you want to be influential, you've got to be willing to look within yourself and ask why. Is it so that you can achieve great things? Is it so that you can enrich the lives of others around you? Do you want to command respect and get things done? Or are you purely interested in making your own life better? Do you see people as a tool to be used, or as friends to be empowered and built upon? Influence depends greatly on your own motivations. Why is that? Well, it's because people can usually tell what your motives are, even if you think you can hide them.

People are hard to motivate unless they are able to understand why something will benefit them. If you want to be influential, it means you have to learn how to communicate to others in such a way that it will convince them that the best thing they can do for themselves is to follow your direction. In other words, they must believe that following after you is a good decision. They must believe they are getting something out of it. And here's the kicker: you must be willing to deliver on what you promise.

The core of being influential in other people's lives is something known as vision.

Vision is an idea that you present to other people. When you have clarity of vision, when you are able to fully convey your vision to others, they will often respond to it, if the vision is in line with what they are a looking for. Great leaders in history have all had extremely clear visions, not only did they have extremely clear visions, they also had visions that other people wanted to be a part of. Usually the vision was something grand like "We're going to build a new country!" or "We're going to set the slaves free!" Some visions were religious "we're going to build a strong church community!" and other visions might have been considered to be controversial "We're going to protest the government!" But all of these visions all had one thing in common: it spoke to the needs and ideas of the people. These visions are so powerful, that those who hear them are driven to be a part of it. In other words, people are influenced more by the vision than they are by the person.

This is why organizations can be so effective at influencing large groups of people. The idea of the single, charismatic cult leader controlling the people with his very charisma is somewhat of a myth. The reality is that everyone in an organization is there of their own free will because on some level, the vision being conveyed to them appeals to their desires. The cult leader is able to sway a group of people not because they are weak willed or dumb, but because the vision that he is sharing with them motivates them greatly. If the vision is especially strong enough, it can even begin to convince people to accept or tolerate things that are harmful in order to achieve it.

So, in summation, if you want to be influential, you must realize that a big part of that influence is being able to convey the right kind of vision to people. You must also be willing to take a hard look at yourself and ask yourself why you want to be influential. Your motives tend to influence your own personal vision. If your motives aren't particularly healthy or good, it can be very hard to exert any kind of influence over others. Many men are willing to fight in a war for their patriotism, love of country or even desire for a paycheck, but no man is willing to die just so that their leader can look good.

Let's be honest, there are definitely people in this world who have learned how to craft effective visions in order to trick people into doing their bidding, as many cult leaders or insane dictators have done, but those kinds of people don't achieve greatness. They go down in history in infamy. If you want to be influential in a good way, if you want to do great things, then you've got to be willing to care about the wellbeing of others. The more that you care, the easier it is to not only craft effective visions that can motivate people, it's also easier for people to understand your own motivations. True loyalty is earned, not bought, and the more that you care about those you are working with, the more they will care about you. This makes it easier to establish long lasting relationships with people who are willing to follow after you.

So, we've established that the best way to motivate people is to create a strong vision that they will respond to. What exactly goes into a vision? Well, let's look at a few different parts of what it means to create a vision, step by step.

Vision Crafting Step One: Figure Out The Message

The first step to being able to sufficiently craft a vision is to understand what kind of message that you are trying to convey. Regardless of whether you are trying to become personally or professionally more influential, it's important to know that without a message, there is no chance of a vision working. A professional message might look like "let's build a great company!" and a personal message might look like "let's build a strong marriage!"

Oftentimes we make the error of thinking way too small when it comes to guiding and leading other people. We usually think in very simple terms and then we get small returns as a result of our thinking small. If you want to achieve great things in life, then you're going to have to have a killer message to convey. You might be someone who has multiple areas where you want to be influential in, such as in your friendships, at work and at church. You might need to craft multiple messages depending on each one, but if you make the mistake of thinking that something is too small for a vision, then you will never get to explore the full potential of the situation.

True influence is really about learning how to affect other people in such a way that it brings out the best in them while simultaneously diminishing the worst in them. A true influencer is someone who can make a person feel strong, confident and secure, while reducing or eliminating their pettiness, frustration or desire to get into squabbles. Can you effectively craft a message that will inspire people to see you as an authority? That will get people to be interested in what you are trying to achieve?

Consider how influential Apple Computers was back in the heyday of Steve Job's career. What was their message to the world? Was the message "buy our stuff?" Not at all! Their message was "we create great products and we believe in innovation beyond all other things." This meant that they conveyed to their customer base that they were cutting edge, hip and interested in making the very best product. This desire for innovation was clear as the way they pioneered a lot of things like the smartphone and the iPod. People caught onto the vision of Apple and responded to the message, becoming dedicated to the brand, sometimes for life. This turned a customer into a follower and greatly affected the way Apple achieved success.

Vision Crafting Step Two: Purpose

Once you've toyed around the idea of what kind of message you are trying to convey, you must then consider what the goal or purpose of the vision is. A purpose is essentially your goal, it is the reason for your vision existing. Are you trying to lead a team to creating an interesting new product? Then the purpose would be making the product. Are you trying to get a group of people to invest in your company? Then you must be able to tell them what the purpose of your company is.

People are deeply connected to a sense of purpose in this world. Everyone is looking for some kind of meaning. It is, in fact, very easy to find lots of people who have no idea of what their purpose is, but they are looking for it. These kinds of people are very easy to motivate, all you have to do is properly convey to them your purpose and if it is to their liking, if it makes sense to them, they will latch onto that sense of purpose.

The reality is that the world is full of people who are skilled and capable of doing incredible things, but most of them lack a clear understanding of what their purpose is. By providing those people with a sense of purpose, you are greatly appealing to their desire for meaning and are frankly doing them a service. Which brings us to our next step.

Vision Crafting Step Three: How

Once you know what your message and purpose is, you must then figure out how you want to implement your vision. Having a sufficient why is very important, but without having a how, your vision won't really be worth anything. Remember, the purpose of the vision is to bring people into being willing to act on your behalf, so you'll need to have action as part of your vision.

Nothing is worse than hearing a leader talk about his grand vision or idea for something but not have a plan. Those kinds of people tend to be seen as nothing more than empty headed dreamers who will never get anything done. If you're going to convey some grand idea to your people, then you must have some kind of idea backing it up. If you want your family to be strong, healthy and spiritual, then you should have a concrete plan on how to achieve that. If you want to get your company to place of financial success, then you must show the people that you know what you are doing.

Your plan doesn't have to be perfect, but it has to exist in order to get people to follow after you. General George S. Patton once said that "a good plan executed immediately is better than a perfect plan executed ten minutes later." The reality is that plans change as you go along, they don't have to be the best but they have to at least exist. It's far easier to make course corrections as you move along than it is to just sit around and wait for something to just fall in your lap.

When you combine these three elements together, you essentially get a vision that should be big, powerful and inviting. You might need a few different visions depending on which areas that you are wanting to influence people in, but be certain that you are going to need a vision. Once you have a vision, what is the next step? Well, you'll need to be able to convey your vision to others and you do that through communication.

Chapter 3: Communicating Influence

So now that we have handled the understanding and internal portions of influence, we must now begin to set our sights on the topic of learning how to actively influence other people. We are capable of influencing others by using the power of communication. Simply put, communication is the art of transmitting ideas or concepts to other people. We often communicate two different ways:

Verbal:

Speech is a form of explicit communication. When we talk to someone, when we use words, we are communicating to them fully aware of exactly what we are saying to them.

Nonverbal:

A big part of the way we communicate to people is through nonverbal cues. Gestures, posture, facial expressions, these are all different ways that we convey thoughts and ideas to people without having to state it. Many times, this can betray our words. We might say "I'm so glad to see you!" but our body language might be drawn back and closed off. People are extremely sensitive to nonverbal communication and can be influenced by it.

These two types of communication will be crucial when it comes to learning how to influence people. Those who are unable to speak clearly will be forever unable to get their vision across to others, while those who aren't able to stop glaring or frowning while talking may end up isolating or alienating the people that they are trying to talk to.

We use the word Charisma to sum up the concept of being able to be seen as appealing or influential to people through our own force of personality. Charisma is a necessary piece of the puzzle, but it is used to compliment a strong vision, not replace it. A person cannot achieve great things through charisma alone, but at the same time, if you want to learn how to communicate your vision clearly, then you are going to need to have some level of charisma.

Some people are naturally more charismatic than others, but this does not mean that just because you aren't silver-tongued doesn't mean you can't influence others in your life. There are fundamentals when it comes to communication, just like any other thing in life. If you spend time learning the fundamentals of communication, how to speak well and how to manage your physical presence, you will be considered to be a charismatic individual. The reality is that most people tend to just lack the social skills that would make them charismatic. All you'd need to do to become better at this is spend some time learning the hallmarks of good communication and then dedicating time to practicing them. Let's look at each piece of good communication step by step so that you can learn how to become more influential.

Communication Principle One: Respect

One of the old adages says, you've got to give respect in order to get it. Yet, this adage isn't particularly helpful due to the fact that it creates entitlement in many people, as they are expecting that other people should be treating them with respect automatically. The reality is that if you want respect, then you must learn how to be respectful with no expectation of getting it back. This will help you immensely when it comes to dealing with those who will be disrespectful to you no matter what.

Respect is one of the foundational principles of communication because it allows for you to treat others with kindness, love and above all, dignity. Now, respect doesn't mean that you have to agree with what everyone tells you, it doesn't mean that you are some kind of doormat who lets people walk all over you. Someone who is respectful can also be strong and assertive, but respect colors how much you genuinely care about other people.

How does it feel when someone respects you and your words? It feels pretty good, doesn't it? Well, when you think about everyone's basic ideas and motivations, you must realize that just about everyone out there desires to be treated with respect and love. By giving someone the respect that they feel like they deserve, they will think better of you and in the process, your influence with them will grow.

So, what are some practical ways that you can learn how to communicate with respect? Well, the first step is to learn that it requires some level of discipline to make sure you treat everyone right. Sometimes there can be a lot of emotion that goes into our decision making and we can be prone to assume that other people are idiots, stupid or that they are somehow beneath us. It takes discipline and humility to be willing to look at another human being and realize that maybe there isn't anything wrong with them. It takes love to even think that perhaps we might be the problem in our situation.

So, on a practical level, we must look at respect as an approach based system of communication. What I mean by approach based is that respect is all about how you approach a situation. For example, if you are trying to handle a conflict at work, you have the option to be disrespectful or respectful, even in the midst of an argument or a fight. What sounds more respectful? "You need to shut up before I make you!" or "I'm sorry that you feel that way, but I don't feel you are being appropriate right now."

The key to respectful communication involves:

- **Looking for solutions, not making accusations**
- **Considering the other person's feelings, emotions and path of life that led them to make this decision**

- **Addressing a person with kindness and not anger**
- **Putting the other individual first**
- **Waiting for the other person to calm down rather than push an issue**
- **Realizing that you are no better than the other person**

The more respect you have for people in general, the more influence and loyalty you will command because people will respond to those who are respectful. However, don't make the mistake of thinking that being weak is being respectful. There are times when you need to put your foot down, or else other people will begin to perceive you as a doormat and that will ultimately lower your influence. Learning how to be respectful but firm is part of the balance necessary to become an exceptionally influential person, which brings us to our next point.

Communication Principle Two: Firmness

Have you ever heard the words "Firm but fair?" Those words are often used to describe those who are able to put their foot down when they need to, but aren't overly aggressive. A person who is firm but fair is often someone who is capable of listening to all sides of the argument before making a judgment. You want to be seen as a respectful individual, but you also need to be seen as someone who is firm and assertive. If you lack the ability to hold to your standards, to say no, to stick to your guns in the face of opposition, then you essentially lack the ability to influence people for very long.

When it comes to looking at leaders, people can tolerate a cruel leader, they can tolerate a mean one and they will usually tolerate a domineering one, but no one likes a weak leader. People will, on a subconscious level, come to resent a leader that they perceive as weak. This isn't permission to become tyrannical or nasty as a leader, but it must make you stop and consider the benefits of being firm with others.

Firmness is often seen as meanness, but there is a purpose behind being firm. When you make the choice not to bend on a decision, to stick to your principles or to argue a point that you know you are right on, you are making a stand based on your conviction. If you are able to do this healthily and respectfully, people will come to respect you for your strength of will.

Many times, people can convince themselves that they are being polite, when the reality is that they are just being a doormat. There is a place and a time for humility, but when it comes to standing up for your own rights or for the rights of those whom you love, then you must be willing to stand up and stand firm. Not saying anything can be problematic if you truly are in the right. So why is it that we aren't always as firm as we need to be? Honestly, it's because we are often giving in to our own fear.

When it comes to conflict, fear tends to be the major factor in what keeps a person from speaking their own mind. They are afraid of being treated poorly, saying the wrong thing, getting punished or worse, they are just afraid of conflict. If you want to be an influential person, then you must be willing to understand that fear is a natural part of human life and you must be willing to overcome that fear in order to do the harder things in life. If you spend your whole life holding back from saying what you really think because you are afraid, you aren't going to be very influential at all.

Think about it like this, without fear you could never have courage. Not everyone has a necessarily aggressive temperament, some people are extremely laid back or timid by nature and thusly it can be harder for them to be assertive when they need to be. Worse yet, many people with a gentler temperament will look at someone who is mean and nasty and assume that they are that way because they are being unbending about a situation or a subject, when the reality is that person would be mean regardless of what they were doing.

How many of us hide behind the excuse of saying "oh I'm not a bully!" or "I don't like to cause problems" when in reality we are actually just trying to avoid the responsibility of handling problems with firmness and authority. There are no points in this life for getting all the way to the grave without upsetting anyone. If you are going to be a leader, someone who desires to be influential and get people to follow after you, then you must realize that there will be times when you will butt heads. If you immediately roll, if you run and hide, no one will have confidence in you as a leader and in the end, it will destroy any chances that you once had of commanding respect and loyalty from your people.

Communication Principle Three: Directness

Perhaps one of the worst traits of our current modern culture is that it seems that as the years have passed, we have begun to master the art of being indirect. People seem very afraid to talk directly about their feelings, about the problem at hand or speak their minds in a way that is honest and fair. Instead, it seems that most people dance around the subject, try to avoid offending people or otherwise are unable to just be straightforward with others. If you want to get ahead in your ability to communicate, then you're going to want to learn how to be direct with others.

Directness is essentially the ability to look someone in the eye and tell them the truth. You don't necessarily have to be mean or harsh, but it means that at the end of the day that you are able to be intellectually honest with people about what you see. People need to be able to trust their leaders and directness is a big part of that trust.

Politeness has become a code word for cowardice these days. Just like with firmness, we very often try to avoid telling the truth because we don't want to feel uncomfortable about having to say something negative or derogatory to someone's face. The reality is that when we hold back our honest opinions, we are doing a terrible disservice to that individual. Consider, for a moment, the fledgling author. Suppose that a friend of yours were to hand you his new book and asked you to read through it. You read it and it is quite abysmal. What would be the best course of action? It would easy to tell him "oh it was great" and never worry about hurting his feelings, but by doing so you are essentially condemning him to try to release a crappy product that will get him nowhere professionally. The best thing to do would to be honestly and respectfully tell him how bad you felt the book was, not criticizing him as a person nor using incendiary language, but rather telling him what you found wrong. Now, you have no way of knowing how he is going to react. If he's an egotistical jerk, then he's going to get angry with you and tell you that you have no idea what good writing is. If he's a sensitive whiner, he might get all offended and cry about it. If he's humble and hungry, as many people in this world are, then he'll take this criticism as an opportunity to change. You will be doing him a great favor by helping him out this way.

Yet, many of us would rather see a friend go on to make a fool of themselves instead of being direct and honest with them. This is not the trademark of a good leader, this is the trademark of a coward. It is not comfortable to have to tell someone that their work sucks, or that you aren't happy with them, or that they could be doing better with something, but if you are able to deliver it right, then you are doing them a favor, even if they don't feel like it is a favor in the moment. Indeed, many a man and woman have been shaped for the better due to what was perceived as harsh criticism. People will come to respect you and will become better underneath your direction if you are able to effectively deliver criticism.

So, what are some tips to being able to effectively deliver criticism? Here are a few:

- **Focus on the results, not the person. If you levy criticism against the person, they will feel attacked, but if you focus primarily on the thing that they are doing or their process, it will seem less personal.**
- **Make sure to say some nice things about them. Some people prefer to use what's known as the sandwich method, where you start off with something nice, levy your criticism and then finish with something nice.**
- **Offer solutions, don't just complain. If you have a problem with the work or characteristic, have some kind of action step in**

your mind, one that will help them figure out how to work through the issue.

- Consider their emotional state before you begin to criticize. Sometimes a person having a bad day will not handle criticism well, so be cautious with your timing.

- Never demean, ridicule or otherwise use harsh language to make your point. Criticism should be seen as kind, loving and uplifting.

- Don't make assumptions about a person's motives. Most people are usually trying the best they can and it wouldn't be fair for you to loudly declare that "you can do better" without understanding the situation first.

Communication Principle Four: Listening

Many people like to talk, but very few in this world like to listen. You, no doubt, have many things to say and most of those things are very important, but one mistake that many of us make is the assumption that what we have to say is more important than what others have going on. So, when people speak to us, instead of listening to their words intently, we are simply waiting for our turn to talk. So, we plan what we are going to say, we listen on a surface level and when it's our turn to talk, we say what we were going to say, not responding to their words or barely acknowledging them before we start pushing our own agenda or ideas.

The art of good communication is a clear back and forth, but so many of us can become erroneously focused on the speaking part that we forget that half of good communication is *listening*. Learning how to listen is one of the most effective tools that you can have in the communication bucket because it will allow for you to learn what a person's thoughts, hopes and desires are, increase your relationship with them as you learn more about them and most impossibly, make them feel loved and cared about.

Have you ever had to repeat some major news to a friend because they weren't listening when you told them? Perhaps you got a big promotion or maybe you finally launched that product you wanted to launch on Etsy and a few days after telling your friend, they don't seem to remember it at all. How does that make you feel? If you're like most people, it can make you feel somewhat diminished or less important, even though it was never your friend's intention to make you feel that way. What about when a friend or maybe even an acquaintance remembers something important that you had mentioned in passing and asks you about it? How does that make you feel? It usually makes you feel important, loved and heard.

Everyone on a deep level craves to be heard. We all deeply desire connection and the passive nature of communication these days, through texts and email, leave out the sensation of truly being acknowledged. When you put in the extra effort and energy to learn how to listen to what people say and then follow up with them at a later time, you are sending a strong message that says "you are important to me!" Someone who feels heard will care much more about a relationship than someone who feels ignored. If you want to increase your natural sphere of influence, having the ability to listen to what people are saying, actively absorbing their words and being able to recall them at a later point will definitely put you over the top.

So, what is the best way to develop listening skills? Well, it's honestly just a matter of being willing to put your own thoughts, ideas and opinions on hold until you have heard all of what they are saying. Part of learning how to listen well is developing a strong sense of empathy that will allow for you to care about their words and opinions. The more you care about a person, the more you will be able to hear what they have to say and keep it in your heart. Learning how to care more about people isn't the easiest thing in the world, but it is possible. All you need to do is just look at the things about a person that you love and focus on what makes them so awesome to you. The more you are willing to look at other people in a caring lens, the easier it will be for you to listen.

Active listening is a skill that works over time, you can only build it by practicing each day. So, the next time you have a conversation, regardless of what you talk about, try to remember one major detail about the person from the conversation and then make a point to mention it the next time you see them. Make a game out of it, this will allow for you to actively focus on building your listening skills without it having to be humdrum and boring. The better listener that you become, the greater level of influence that you will have on other people's lives.

Communication Principle Five: Body Language

As stated before, there is a major amount of information communicated nonverbally to other people, this is communicated through our body language. Body language is essentially a mixture of posture, physical positioning and facial expressions that convey our thoughts, moods and ideas to other people. Most of the time, we can be unaware of the extreme impact that our body language has on other people. If we are not careful, we might end up sending wrong messages and signals to people through the way our posture is, so if you want to learn how to be a strong communicator then you must be willing to learn the basics of body language control.

The most basic principle when it comes to learning how to manage our body language is to recognize the role that our bodies play when we communicate. Think about how you know someone is angry, for instance. How does an angry person stand? How do they sit? Usually there's some kind of tenseness in their arms and chest, they might be leaning forward aggressively and there might be a furrowed brow, clenching of teeth, agitation in their voice. It's incredibly easy to tell when someone is angry if they aren't controlling how they appear, but how many times have you met someone who was angry but doing their best to conceal their anger? They might appear relaxed to the eye, they might be drawn back and casual, but there is still something that radiates anger from them. Maybe it's in their eyes, or perhaps their voice, but on some subconscious level, we know that this person is angry. This is because the human brain is able to piece several different cues together to create an idea, while we might not consciously understand why we feel a person is mad, our brain is able to figure it out.

This means that if we are going to learn how to influence other people, we must focus not only on delivering a message with our words, but also with our bodies. The human brain is designed to watch how other bodies act in order to determine many different things, and we can take advantage of this as well. By learning to focus on how we are presenting ourselves, we can either detract from or enhance our message. Good posture and emoting can make your message much more valuable, while bad posture and poor display of facial expressions may end up taking away from what you are trying to convey. Don't ever let your message be undermined by your body.

The first step in learning how to use your body to back up your words is to learn how to be mindful of your posture and your presence. Posture is probably one of the most important parts of body language because it will indicate to people how comfortable you are in this situation. If your chest is puffed out and you are confident, then people will assume that you are confident about your words, even if you aren't! Yet, if your chest was sunken, your back was slouched and you were looking at the ground, you might be perceived as lying, making things up, being uncomfortable or just simply not knowing what you are talking about.

Imagine your body like an outfit. What outfit would you put on for an important job interview? Would you wear a pair of slacks and a ratty t-shirt, or would you wear a suit? You would want to dress in a way that would have an impact on the person that you are trying to win over. So, when it comes to adjusting our body language, we need to realize that our body is more or less like a good suit in a job interview. This means that you must be willingly to "dress up" so to speak when it comes time to deliver important messages to people.

Don't underestimate the power of posture. When you stand up straight, keep your chest out, hang your head high and make frequent eye contact, you are signaling to others that you are confident, strong and trustworthy. Eye contact is especially one of the most important parts of the body language puzzle, because it allows for you to connect to people on an intimate level. Let's take a look at each part of your body and the role that it plays during communication.

Head:

The head shows where the attention of a person is directed. Someone who is staring at the ground or up at the ceiling shows that they aren't paying much attention. Someone who's staring just at one single person during a speech or conversation with a group will cause that individual to feel very uncomfortable. Instead of keeping the head in one static area, the best way to use your head during any kind of interaction is to do what's known as scanning. Look around the room in a slow, steady manner, acknowledging all of the people that you are talking to and never staying focused on one person for too long. Don't move your head too quick or you'll look like you struggle with an attention disorder, and don't move too slow because then it will come off as inorganic and somewhat weird. The ideal pace is to just sweep slowly and casually, making eye contact with each person and making sure that no one is left out when you talk. That's the purpose of scanning, it's acknowledging each and every person in the room on a personal basis.

Eye:

Eye contact is extremely important, but be careful with it. Most people want some degree of eye contact, but they don't want to feel stared down or domineered. Try limiting your eye contact to a few seconds each time, but make sure you make frequent eye contact during a conversation. Nothing is more important than looking someone in the eyes and firmly speaking truth to them, it can be a powerful accent to your message. Eye contact is usually perceived as a sign of honesty hand having nothing to hide, so always make an effort to do so.

Arms:

The arms are an interesting part of the body language system because they can be used to signal all sorts of different things to people. Placing your arms on your hips causes you to look angry or annoyed, swinging your arms or idly touching things causes you to look bored or inattentive. One interesting trick is that crossing your arms is actually considered to be a sign of liking someone. If you cross your arms and the person you are talking to cross their arms too, it is a sign that they are comfortable and like you. Sometimes crossing arms can be a signal of aggression or it can be the act of making yourself seem larger than you really are, as a defensive posture.

Torso:

A straight back and a puffed-out chest indicates confidence. A slouch shows that you aren't particularly fearsome or that you are immensely uncomfortable with the situation at hand. There are literally no reasons for you to keep a low profile unless you are trying to avoid having attention on you, so make sure that you focus on learning how to keep your back straight, your head high and your chest puffed out.

Legs:

Your stance can essentially determine how open you are to other people. If your toes are pointing inward and you have taken a step back from a person, it can be seen as a very defensive and closed off position. If your feet are pointed outwards, it is an inviting signal and it can allow other people to feel at ease coming into your circle. Proximity is also another point to consider as well. The closer that you get to someone, the more intimate the spacing becomes. If you are good friends with someone, proximity can be a good thing, but the traditional American values tend to keep other people at somewhat of a distance, so make sure that you aren't making someone feel uncomfortable by getting to close to them. It's a tough balance but you can generally tell how comfortable people are with your distance based on the way that they move away from you. Don't follow them if they move back a little bit, instead take that as a sign of discomfort.

Breath:

Yes, it's true that breath can also have an effect on your communication level. It's not necessarily a deal breaker, but if you focus on improving your breath and making sure that it is minty fresh, you will be potentially avoiding a bad deal. One reason why breath can stink, even after you brush, is because you aren't effectively taking care of your tongue area. The tongue carries more bacteria and enzymes than the teeth do, so by neglecting to brush your tongue, you are essentially contributing to worse breath. The best way to clean your tongue is to either buy yourself one of those fancy tongue brushes or if you're low budget, you could just use a spoon to scrape your tongue each morning. This is an incredibly effective way to decrease breath issues throughout the day and by doing so, you are increasing your ability to communicate well to others.

Chapter 4: Extreme Influence

Hopefully by this point you've come to realize that influence is more of a culmination of a series of efforts to improve your communication, understand your fellow man and most importantly, learning how to convey your vision. Once you've realized that these are the things that will ultimately make you more influential, it's time to look at a few different tips and tricks out that there that you can use to increase your personal level of influence. Remember, without a proper foundation, there is very little chance of you being able to increase your level of influence with these tips, so use them as a supplement as you grow in areas of understanding, vision crafting and communication. Let's take a look.

Influence Increaser 1: Dress for Success

How you dress can often have a subtle yet effective way to influence the people around you. By dressing sharp, taking care of your hair and facial hair, you will be able to convey the message that you care about yourself. In doing so, you are communicating to people that you are someone who is in charge of your own life and people will respond to that. A well-dressed man will almost always command more respect than a man wearing some ratty clothing. Of course, don't mistake the art of dressing well as an excuse for behaving poorly. There are many men wearing expensive and fancy suits who will have no influence in life because their behavior is terrible. Try to blend the best of both worlds, dress well and live well.

Influence Increaser 2: Be Positive

Positive people tend to be far more well received than negative ones. A person with a perpetual frown won't make as big of an impact as someone who walks with a skip in their step and a song on their lips. This isn't an excuse to be fake and pretend that you are happy when you aren't, but it is an invitation to make a concrete effort to focus on the positive things in life. People who smile more, laugh more and are capable of looking for the good in everything tend to be perceived as happier and better leaders, so don't be an eyesore!

Influence Increaser 3: Be Funny

One of the best ways to get people to like you is to learn how to tell jokes and have a sense of humor. People who can't laugh at themselves or take themselves too seriously are extremely off-putting and will never command the same level of respect and admiration as someone who is kind and funny. People with a sense of humor will always have a leg up from a humorless stick in the mud. At the same time, it's important to make sure that you aren't over funny either, everyone likes a class clown but few people will trust him. It's important to have balance between those two worlds and make sure you don't fall too much in either one category.

Influence Increaser 4: Apologize

If you ever end up in the wrong, it is extremely important for you to be able to apologize to your people. A leader who refuses to admit that he is wrong will quickly lose the respect from his colleagues and worst of all, he will be perceived as a jerk who doesn't really care about his own people. If you were wronged, you would expect an apology, so it would make sense that if you were to wrong someone then you should make it right to them. Leaders who apologize are seen as more trustworthy, sincere and honest than those who refuse to admit failures and mistakes.

Influence Increaser 5: Bring the Energy

If you want to influence a crowd, group of people or just a sales staff, then you are going to need to be willing to set the pace. The more energetic and excited that you are, the easier it is to motivate others. People tend to respond to the highest energy in the room, so if you are low key, relaxed and mumbly, they won't respond with high levels of energy. On the flipside, if you focus on being an energy carrier, you will be able to set the pace for the people around you. Someone who is high energy is infectious and it will spread to others. Be the change that you want to see in your group.

Influence Increaser 6: Be Vulnerable

The idea of the fearless, emotionless leader who never shows weakness or pain is a myth. Everyone has personal problems, everyone has struggles going on in their lives and it would be ridiculous for you to try and create the image that you don't have any problems. People empathize with leaders and bosses who are seen as more human and being seen as human requires that you be vulnerable. This isn't to mean that you should throw out all of your problems in front of everyone to see, but it does require you to have a certain level of honesty about what's going on in your life to the people you are around. The more vulnerable you can be as a leader, the more trustworthy you will be seen. When people trust you, they will listen to your direction much easier than if they were suspicious of you. Vulnerability is key to gaining that trust.

Influence Increaser 7: Praise Often

A good leader is someone who is constantly uplifting, encouraging and praising his followers. If you are trying to get the best out of people in your life, then you must be willing to praise them on a consistent basis. Don't be a flatterer however, focus on praising people only on the achievements that they are actually making. Flattery is insincere and wants something, but praise is genuine and only wants to recognize people for their accomplishments. If a person feels recognized for something that they did, no matter how small, it will make them feel good and it will boost their morale. Praise cost nothing but a few moments to acknowledge a person's good deeds and it will reap fantastic rewards, so don't be a cheapskate when it comes to doling out praise to those who deserve it.

Influence Increaser 8: Be Ethical

It is extremely easy to cut corners in life. You can ignore a few laws here, skip paying for some licenses there and soon enough, you've built an entire life out of not paying attention to the rules that everyone else is required to play by. If your people see you as someone who acts unethically, it will create tension between them and you. They will see you as a liar, a cheat and a thief and will be constantly worried about your actions and how it might affect them. You want your people to feel at ease as you lead and influence them in their lives, and the fastest way to erode that sense of trust and safety is to show them that you only follow the rules when it benefits you. You must be willing to make an extreme commitment to ethics so that you can be held up as blameless in the eyes of those who admire and follow after you.

Influence Increaser 9: Availability

Perhaps one of the strongest ways to signal that you care about someone is to be available to them no matter what. This means that you have an open-door policy if you are the boss, it means that you are willing to reply promptly to text messages and emails and it means that when someone needs to meet with you, you should make a general effort to be able to meet with them. Someone who is constantly busy is often seen as neglectful and if you are always avoiding meeting with someone, eventually they will come to think that you don't feel that they are important. Now, it's important that you don't get overloaded with too many meetings, but you should honestly be making a reasonable attempt to be available to those whom you lead.

Conclusion

Influence is not magic. It is quite simply a series of principles and foundations that if followed, will result in you naturally being able to command the admiration, love and respect of the people around you. Being an influential person requires vision, it requires the ability to care deeply about others and most importantly, it requires you being willing to do the hard work in order to win people over to your cause. If you follow the principles of this book, if you focus on crafting a strong vision, learning how to communicate and stay focused on serving people as best as you can, then you will find that you will become an extremely influential person. You can honestly change the world, as long as you are in it for the right reasons. People can sniff inauthenticity from a mile away, so keep in mind that anything that you want to achieve, it needs to be for a greater cause than just self-enhancement. You can become a great influencer, you can change the world. All you need to do is show people that you care enough and they will follow.

Other books available by Landon T. Smith on Kindle, paperback and audio:

How to Outmaneuver And Outsmart Anyone: Time Tested Strategies That Will Give You the Upper Hand When Dealing With People

How to Develop, Build and Increase Your Momentum